Penguin Modern European Poets D114
Advisory Editor: A. Alvarez

Vasko Popa · Selected Poems

Vasko Popa was born in 1922 in Grebenac, Banat
(Yugoslavia). He studied at the universities of
Vienna, Bucharest and Belgrade, taking his degree
in French and Yugoslav literature in Belgrade in
1949. He now works as editor at the Nolit
publishing house in Belgrade.

Four collections of his poems have been
published: *Kora* (Bark), *Nepočin-Polje* (Unrest-
Field), *Pesme* (Poems) and *Sporedno Nebo*
(Secondary Heaven). He has received a number
of literary awards, including the Branko
Radičević prize (1953), the Zmaj prize (1956), and
the Lenau prize (1967). His poems have been
translated into French, German, Rumanian,
Czech, Slovak, Polish and Hungarian, and some
have been set to music by Dušan Radić and
Milko Kelemen.

Vasko Popa
Selected Poems

Translated by
Anne Pennington

With an Introduction by
Ted Hughes

Penguin Books

guin Books Ltd, Harmondsworth,
dlesex, England
nguin Books Australia Ltd, Ringwood,
ictoria, Australia

First published 1969
Copyright © Vasko Popa, 1952, 1956, 1965, 1968
Translation copyright © Anne Pennington, 1969
Introduction copyright © Ted Hughes, 1967

Made and printed in Great Britain by
Hunt Barnard & Co. Ltd, Aylesbury
Set in Monotype Bembo

The poems in this selection are taken from the
following books, to whose publishers acknowledge-
ment is made: *Kora* (1952), *Nepočin-Polje* (1956), *Pesme*
(1965), *Sporedno Nebo* (1968) by Vasko Popa.
Anne Pennington would like to thank the author and
Olga Stefanović for their invaluable assistance in these
translations.

Contents

from SECONDARY HEAVEN (1968)

The yawn of yawns

Signs

Dissension

Imitation of the sun

Introduction to the poetry of Vasko Popa

Vasko Popa is a Yugoslav and was born in 1922. He studied literature at the University of Belgrade and now works in a publishing house. His published books of verse are *Kora* (1952), *Nepočin-Polje* (1956), *Pesme* (1965) and *Sporedno Nebo* (1968).

He is one of a generation of East European poets – Holub of Czechoslovakia and Herbert of Poland are perhaps two others of similar calibre – who were caught in mid-adolescence by the war. Their reaction to the mainly surrealist principles that prevailed in Continental poetry in the inter-war years was a matter of personal temperament, but it has been reinforced by everything that has since happened, to their countries in particular and in some measure (more than ever before) to human beings everywhere. Circumstantial proof that man is a political animal, a state numeral, as if it needed to be proved, has been weighed out in dead bodies by the million. The attempt these poets are making to put on record that man is also, at the same time and in the same circumstances, an acutely conscious human creature of suffering and hope, has brought their poetry down to such precisions, discriminations and humilities that it is a new thing. It seems closer to the common reality, in which we have to live if we are to survive, than to those other realities in which we can holiday, or into which we decay when our bodily survival is comfortably taken care of, and which art, particularly contemporary art, is forever trying to impose on us as some sort of superior dimension. I think it was Miłosz, the Polish poet, who when he lay in a doorway and watched the bullets lifting the cobbles out of the street beside him realized that most poetry is not equipped for life in a world

9

where people actually do die. But some is. And the poets of whom Popa is one seem to have put their poetry to a similar test.

We can guess at the forces which shaped their outlook and style. They have had to live out, in actuality, a vision which for artists elsewhere is a prevailing shape of things but only brokenly glimpsed, through the clutter of our civilized liberal confusion. They must be reckoned among the purest and most wide awake of living poets.

In a way, their world reminds one of Beckett's world. Only theirs seems braver, more human, and so more real. It is as horrible as his but they do not despair of it to the point of surrendering consciousness and responsibility to their animal cells. Their poetic themes revolve around the living suffering spirit, capable of happiness, much deluded, too frail, with doubtful and provisional senses, so undefinable as to be almost silly, but palpably existing, and wanting to go on existing – and this is not, as in Beckett's world, absurd. It is the only precious thing, and designed in accord with the whole universe. Designed, indeed, by the whole universe. They are not the spoiled brats of civilization disappointed of impossible and unreal expectations and deprived of the revelations of necessity. In this they are prophets speaking somewhat against their times, though in an undertone, and not looking for listeners. They have managed to grow up to a view of the unaccommodated universe, but it has not made them cynical, they still like it and keep all their sympathies intact. They have got back to the simple animal courage of accepting the odds.

In another way, their world reminds one of the world of modern physics. Only theirs is more useful to us, in that while it is the same gulf of unknowable laws and unknowable particles, the centre of gravity is not within some postulate deep in space, or leaking away down the drill-shaft of mathematics, but inside man's sense of himself, inside his body and his essential human subjectivity, his refusal to surrender his individuality to any impersonal abstraction, political or fashionable or whatever. They refuse to sell out their arms, legs, hair, ears, body and soul and all it has suffered with them, in order to escape with some fragmentary sense, some abstract badge of self-estrangement, into a popular membership safety. They accept in a sense what the prisoner must accept, who cannot pretend that any finger is at large. Like men come back from the dead they have an improved perception, an unerring sense of what really counts in being alive.

This helplessness in the circumstances has purged them of rhetoric. They cannot falsify their experience by any hopeful effort to change it. Their poetry is a strategy of making audible meanings without disturbing the silence, an art of homing in tentatively on vital scarcely perceptible signals, making no mistakes, but with no hope of finality, continuing to explore. Finally, with delicate manoeuvring, they precipitate out of a world of malicious negatives a happy positive. And they have created a small ironic space, a work of lyrical art, in which their humanity can respect itself.

Vasko Popa uses his own distinctive means. Like the others, he gives the impression of being well-acquainted with all that civilization has amassed in the way of hypotheses. Again, like the others, he seems to have played the film of history over to himself many times. Yet he has been thoroughly stripped of any spiritual or mental proprietorship. No poetry could carry less luggage than his, or be freer of predisposition and preconception. No poetry is more difficult to outflank, yet it is in no sense defensive. His poems are trying to find out what does exist, and what the conditions really are. The movement of his verse is part of his method of investigating something fearfully apprehended, fearfully discovered. But he will not be frightened into awe. He never loses his deeply ingrained humour and irony: that is his way of hanging on to his human wholeness. And he never loses his intense absorption in what he is talking about, either. His words test their way forward, sensitive to their own errors, dramatically and intimately alive, like the antennae of some rock-shore creature feeling out the presence of the sea and the huge powers in it. This analogy is not so random. There is a primitive pre-creation atmosphere about his work, as if he were present where all the dynamisms and formulae were ready and charged, but nothing created – or only a few fragments. Human beings, as visibly and wholly such, do not appear in Popa's landscapes. Only heads, tongues, spirits, hands, flames, magically vitalized wandering objects, such as apples and moons, present themselves, animated with strange but strangely familiar destinies. His poetry is near the world of music, where a repository of selected signs and forms, admitted from the outer world, act out fundamental combinations that often have something eerily mathematical about their progressions and symmetries, but which seem to belong deeply to the world of spirit or of the heart. Again like music, his poems turn the most grisly confrontations into something deadpan playful: a spell, a riddle, a game, a story.

He arrived at this freedom and inevitability gradually. His earliest manner often owes a lot to a familiar kind of mildly surrealist modern poesy, though it is charming in Popa, and already purposeful, as in the poem titled 'In forgetting', which is from a series of landscapes:

From the distant darkness
The plain stuck out its tongue
The uncontrollable plain

Spilt events
Spent faded words
Levelled faces

Here and there
A hand of smoke

Sighs without oars
Thoughts without wings
Homeless glances

Here and there
A flower of mist

Unsaddled shadows
More and more quietly paw
The hot ash of laughter

That is from his first book, *Kora*, but 'Acquaintance'' the
first poem in the same book, already sketches out the essential
method and universe of his much later and more character-
istic work:

Don't try to seduce me blue vault
I'm not playing
You are the vault of the thirsty palate
Over my head

Ribbon of space
Don't wind round my legs
Don't try to entrance me
You are a wakeful tongue
A seven-forked tongue
Beneath my steps
I'm not coming

My ingenuous breathing
My breathless breathing
Don't try to intoxicate me
I sense the breath of the beast
I'm not playing

I hear the familiar clash of dogs
The clash of teeth on teeth
I feel the dark of the jaws
That opens my eyes
I see

I see
I'm not dreaming

It is all there, the surprising fusion of unlikely elements.
The sophisticated philosopher is also a primitive, gnomic
spellmaker. The desolate view of the universe opens through
eyes of childlike simplicity and moody oddness. The wide
perspective of general elemental and biological law is spelled
out with folklore hieroglyphs and magical monsters. The
whole style is a marvellously effective artistic invention. It
enables Popa to be as abstract as man can be, yet remain as
intelligible and entertaining and as fully human as if he were
telling a comic story. It is in this favourite device of his, the
little fable of visionary anecdote, that we see most clearly his
shift from literary surrealism to the far older and deeper
thing, the surrealism of folklore. The distinction between
the two seems to lie in the fact that literary surrealism is
always connected with an extreme remove from the business of living under practical difficulties and successfully
managing them. The mind, having abandoned the struggle
with circumstances and consequently lost the unifying
focus that comes of that, has lost morale and surrendered to

the arbitrary imagery of the dream flow. Folktale surrealism, on the other hand, is always urgently connected with the business of trying to manage practical difficulties so great that they have forced the sufferer temporarily out of the dimension of coherent reality into that depth of imagination where understanding has its roots and stores its X-rays. There is no sense of surrender to the dream flow for its own sake or of relaxation from the outer battle. In the world of metamorphoses and flights the problems are dismantled and solved, and the solution is always a practical one. This type of surrealism, if it can be called surrealism at all, goes naturally with a down-to-earth, alert tone of free inquiry, and in Popa's poetry the two appear everywhere together.

The air of trial and error exploration, of an improvised language, the attempt to get near something for which he is almost having to invent the words in a total disregard for poetry or the normal conventions of discourse, goes with his habit of working in cycles of poems. He will trust no phrase with his meaning for more than six or seven words at a time before he corrects his tack with another phrase from a different direction. In the same way, he will trust no poem with his meaning for more than fifteen or so lines, before he tries again from a totally different direction with another poem. Each cycle creates the terms of a universe, which he then explores, more or less methodically, with the terms. And one of the attractions of all Popa's poems is that one cannot set any limit to how deeply into the substance of the universe his intuitions may penetrate. The cycle called *Games*, for instance, is close to mankind as we know it. Nothing prevents these poems from being merely ingenious, or virtuoso pieces of phrasing and timing, except the shock of recognition they impart, and the universe of grim evil which they evoke. It could as well be protozoa, or mathematical possibilities, playing these games, as anything in humanity. They are deeper than our reality as puppets are deeper than our reality: the more human they look and act the more elemental they seem.

In his latest collection, *Secondary Heaven* (1968), the total vision is vast and one understands why he has been called an epic poet. His cosmos is more mysteriously active and dreadful but his affection for our life is closer than ever. The infinite terrible circumstances that seem to destroy man's importance, appear as the very terms of his importance. Man is the face, arms, legs etc. grown over the infinite, terrible All. Popa's poems work in the sanity and fundamental simplicity of this fact, as it might appear to a man sitting in a chair.

TED HUGHES

from BARK (1952)

List

Duck

She waddles through the dust
In which no fish are smiling
Within her sides she carries
The restlessness of water

Clumsy
She waddles slowly
The reeds she's thinking of
She'll reach them anyway

Never
Never will she be able
To walk
As she was able
To plough the mirrors

Horse

Usually
He has eight legs

Between his jaws
Man came to live
From his four corners of earth
Then he bit his lips to blood
He wanted
To chew through that maize stalk
It was all long ago

In his lovely eyes
Sorrow has closed
Into a circle
For the road has no ending
And he must drag behind him
The whole world

Donkey

Sometimes he brays
Rolls in the dust
Sometimes
Then you notice him

Otherwise
You see only his ears
On the head of the planet
But he's not there

Pig

Only when she felt
The savage knife in her throat
Did the red veil
Explain the game
And she was sorry
She had torn herself
From the mud's embrace
And had hurried that evening
From the field so joyfully
Hurried to the yellow gate

Dandelion

On the edge of the pavement
At the end of the world
The yellow eye of loneliness

Blind steps
Beat down his neck
Into the stone belly
Underground elbows
Drive his roots
Into the black earth of the sky
A dog's lifted leg
Mocks him
With an overheated shower
His joy is only
A stroller's homeless glance
Which spends the night
In his corolla
And so
The stub burns out
On the lower lip of impotence
At the end of the world

Far within us

I

We lift our hands
The street climbs up into the sky
We drop our eyes
The roofs descend into the earth

Out of each pain
Which we do not mention
A chestnut tree grows up
And remains mysterious behind us

Out of each hope
Which we cherish
A star arises
And moves unattainable in front of us

Do you hear the shot
Which flies around our head
Do you hear the shot
Which guards our kiss

2

The streets of your glances
Have no ending

The swallows from your eyes
Do not migrate south

From the aspens in your breasts
The leaves do not fall

In the heaven of your words
The sun does not set

3

Our day is a green apple
Cut in two

I look at you
You do not see me
Between us is the blind sun

On the steps
Our torn embrace

You call me
I do not hear you
Between us is the deaf air

In shop windows
My lips are seeking
Your smile

At the crossroads
Our trampled kiss

I have given you my hand
You do not feel it
Emptiness has embraced you

In the squares
Your tear is seeking
My eyes

In the evening my day dead
Meets with your dead day

Only in sleep
We walk the same paths

4

These are your lips
That I return
To your neck

This is my moonlight
That I take down
From your shoulders

We have lost each other
In the impenetrable woods
Of our meeting

In my hands
Your adam's apples
Set and dawn

In your throat
Flame up and fade
My impetuous stars

We have found each other
On the golden plateau
Far within us

Pilgrimage

Sopoćani*

Rosy calm of strength
Mature calm of greatness

From the golden birds below earth
To the profusion of fruit in the heavens
All is within reach

The forms have knelt marvellously
In the eye of the artist

(Time has gnawed at it)

Young beauty of pride
Sleepwalker's certainty

The gates of eternal spring
And the bright weapons of happiness
All wait only for a sign

In the artist's right hand
Beat the pulses of the world

(Time has gnawed at it
And broken its teeth)

*Sopoćani (about 1260-70), Manasija (1406-18) and Kalenić (1407-13) are three of the Serbian monasteries famous for their frescoes.

Manasija

Blue and gold
Last ring of the horizon
Last apple of the sun

Oh Zograf
How far does your sight reach

Do you hear the night horsemen
Allah il ilallah

Your brush does not tremble
Your colours are not afraid

The night horsemen come closer
Allah il ilallah

Oh Zograf
What do you see in the night's depth

Gold and blue
Last star in the soul
Last infinity in the eye

Kalenić

Whence my eyes
In your face
Angel my brother

The colours dawn
On the edge of forgetting

Other shades forbid me
To return the lightning
Of your sword to its sheath

The colours ripen
On the weightless branch of time

Hence your lovely stubbornness
At the corners of my lips
Angel my brother

The colours burn
With youth in my blood

Radimlja*

Amid the pathlessness
An upraised hand
Flamed with its palm
Flashed with its fingers

Long ago it freed
The old native sun
Tied to the tails
Of foreign stallions

Today it illuminates
The cavern of mystery
Hollowed out by questions
In my brow of stone

An upraised hand
Wordless met me
Amid the pathlessness
And showed me the way

*In Bosnia-Hercegovina there are a large number of tombs (commonly held to be Bogomil) with geometric and representational carvings. One at Radimlja shows a man's figure, holding up a disproportionately large hand with outstretched fingers. This has been interpreted as a symbol of the sun.

Belgrade

White bone among the clouds

You arise out of your pyre
Out of your ploughed-up barrows
Out of your scattered ashes

You arise out of your disappearance

The sun keeps you
In its golden reliquary
High above the yapping of the centuries

And carries you to the marriage
Of the fourth river of Paradise
With the thirty-sixth river of Earth

White bone among the clouds
Bone of our bones

UNREST–FIELD (1956)

FOR HASHA

Shall I be able on this unrest-field to set up
for you a tent of my own hands?
                    FAR WITHIN US (1943)

Games

Before play

To Zoran Mišić

One shuts one eye
Peers into oneself into every corner
Looks at oneself to see there are no spikes no thieves
No cuckoos' eggs

One shuts the other eye too
Crouches then jumps
Jumps high high high
To the top of oneself

Thence one drops by one's own weight
For days one drops deep deep deep
To the bottom of one's abyss

He who is not smashed to smithereens
He who remains whole and gets up whole
He plays

The nail

One be the nail another the pincers
The others are workmen

The pincers take the nail by the head
With their teeth with their hands they grip him
And tug him tug
To get him out of the ceiling
Usually they only pull his head off
It's difficult to get a nail out of the ceiling

Then the workmen say
The pincers are no good
They smash their jaws they break their arms
And throw them out of the window

After that someone else be the pincers
Someone else the nail
The others are workmen

Hide-and-seek

Someone hides from someone
Hides under his tongue
He looks for him under the earth

He hides on his forehead
He looks for him in the sky

He hides in his forgetting
He looks for him in the grass

Looks for him looks
Where doesn't he look for him
And looking for him loses himself

The seducer

One caresses the leg of a chair
Until the chair turns
And gives him a welcome sign with its leg

Another kisses a keyhole
Kisses it doesn't he just kiss it
Until the keyhole returns his kiss

A third stands by
Gapes at the other two
And twists his head twists it

Until his head falls off

The wedding

Each takes off his skin
Each uncovers his constellation
Which has never seen the night

Each fills his skin with stones
Each starts dancing with it
By the light of his own stars

He who goes on till dawn
He who doesn't blink doesn't drop
He earns his skin

(This game is rarely played)

The rose thieves

Someone be a rose tree
Some be the wind's daughters
Some the rose thieves

The rose thieves creep up on the rose tree
One of them steals a rose
Hides it in his heart

The wind's daughters appear
See the tree plundered of its beauty
And give chase to the rose thieves

Open up their breasts one by one
In some they find a heart
In some so help me none

They go on opening up their breasts
Until they uncover one heart
And in that heart the stolen rose

Between games

No one is resting

This one keeps moving his eyes about
Puts them on his shoulders
And willy nilly goes backwards
Puts them on the soles of his feet
And again willy nilly comes back headlong

And this one has turned himself altogether into an ear
And heard everything that can't be heard
But he's had enough
And is aching to turn back into himself
But without eyes he can't see how

And that one has uncovered all his faces
And is chasing them one after the other over the roofs
The last he throws underfoot
And buries his head in his hands

And this one has stretched out his look
Stretched it from thumb to thumb
And is walking along it walking
At first slowly afterwards more quickly
And quicker and quicker

And that one is playing with his head
Tosses it up into the air
And catches it on his forefinger
Or doesn't catch it at all

No one is resting

He

Some bite off the others'
Arm or leg or whatever

Take it between their teeth
Run off as quick as they can
Bury it in the earth

The others run in all directions
Sniff search sniff search
Turn up all the earth

If any are lucky enough to find their arm
Or leg or whatever
It's their turn to bite

The game goes on briskly

As long as there are arms
As long as there are legs
As long as there is anything whatever

The seed

Someone sows someone
Sows him in his head
Stamps the earth down well

Waits for the seed to sprout

The seed hollows out his head
Turns it into a mouse hole
The mice eat the seed

There they lie dead

The wind comes to live in the empty head
And gives birth to fickle breezes

Leapfrog*

Two be stones on each other's hearts
Stones like a house
Neither under the stone can budge

And both struggle
At least to lift a finger
At least to click their tongue at least move their ears
Or at least to blink

Neither under the stone can budge

And both struggle
And exhaust themselves and fall asleep from exhaustion
And it's only in their sleep their hair stands on end

(This game lasts a long time)

*'Leapfrog', literally 'Rotten nag'. It is sometimes played like our Leapfrog, but the genuine game is played in teams, as follows. One team of three or four form into the approximate shape of a horse: the first, standing, holds in his linked hands the head of the second, who stoops down. The third puts his head between the second's legs and holds on to his legs. The fourth similarly to the third. Then the members of the second team jump on, trying to land on top of the other on a weak spot, so that they knock the first team over. The first team go on being the 'nag' until they withstand the assault.

The hunter

Someone goes in without knocking
Goes into somebody's one ear
And comes out of the other

Goes in with the step of a match
The step of a lighted match
Dances round inside his head

He's made it

Someone goes in without knocking
Goes into somebody's one ear
And doesn't come out of the other

He's done for

Ashes

Some are nights others stars

Each night lights up its star
And dances a black dance round it
Until the star burns out

Then the nights split up
Some become stars
The others remain nights

Again each night lights up its star
And dances a black dance round it
Until the star burns out

The last night becomes both star and night
It lights itself
Dances the black dance round itself

After play

At last the hands clutch at the stomach
Lest the stomach burst with laughing
But there is no stomach

One hand just manages to lift itself
To wipe the cold sweat from the forehead
There's no forehead either

The other hand reaches to the heart
Lest the heart leap out of the breast
There isn't a heart either

Both hands drop
Idle drop into the lap
There's no lap either

On one hand now the rain is falling
From the other grass is growing
What more should I say

One bone to another

At the beginning

That's better
We've got away from the flesh

Now we will do what we will
Say something

Would you like to be
The backbone of a streak of lightning

Say something more

What should I say to you
Pelvis of a storm

Say something else

I don't know anything else
Ribs of the heavens

We are not anyone's bones
Say something different

After the beginning

What shall we do now

Indeed what shall we do
Now we'll have marrow for supper

We ate the marrow for lunch
Now a hollow feeling is nagging at me

Then we'll make music
We like music

What shall we do when the dogs come
They like bones

Then we'll stick in their throats
And have fun

In the sun

It's marvellous sunbathing naked
I never liked the flesh

I wasn't keen on those rags either
I'm crazy about you naked like this

Don't let the sun caress you
Let's rather love each other just the two of us

Only not here only not in the sun
Here everything can be seen bone darling

Underground

Muscle of darkness muscle of flesh
It comes to the same thing

Well what shall we do now

We'll invite all the bones of all times
We'll bake in the sun

What shall we do then

Then we'll grow pure
Go on growing as we please

What shall we do afterwards

Nothing we'll wander here and there
We'll be eternal beings of bone

Just wait for the earth to yawn

In the moonlight

What's that now
As if flesh some snowy flesh
Were clinging to me

I don't know what it is
As if marrow were running through me
Some cold marrow

I don't know either
As if everything were beginning again
With a more horrible beginning

Do you know what
Can you bark

Before the end

Where shall we go now

Where should we go nowhere
Where would two bones go else

What shall we do there

There long awaiting us
There eagerly expecting us
No one and his wife nothing

What good are we to them

They are old they are without bones
We'll be like daughters to them

At the end

I am a bone you are a bone
Why have you swallowed me
I can't see myself any more

What's wrong with you
It's you have swallowed me
I can't see myself either

Where am I now

Now no one knows any more
Who is where nor who is who
All is an ugly dream of dust

Can you hear me

I can hear both you and myself
There's a cockspur crowing out of us

Give me back my rags

Just come to my mind
And my thoughts will scratch out your face

Just come into my sight
And my eyes will start snarling at you

Just open your mouth
And my silence will smash your jaws

Just remind me of you
And my remembering will paw up the ground under
    your feet

That's what it's come to between us

I

Give me back my rags

My rags of pure dreaming
Of silken smiling of striped foreboding
Of my cloth of lace

My rags of spotted hope
Of burnished desire of mottled glances
Of skin from my face

Give me back my rags
Give me when I ask you nicely

2

Listen you monster
Take off that white scarf
We know each other

Since we were so high
Guzzled from the same bowl

Slept in the same bed
With you evil-eyed knife

Roamed the crooked world
With you snake in the grass

Do you hear dissembler
Take off that white scarf
Why lie to each other

3

I won't take you a pick-a-back
I won't carry you wherever you say

I won't not even shod with gold
Nor harnessed to the wind's three wheeled chariot
Nor bridled with the rainbow's bridle

Don't try to buy me

I won't not even with my feet in my pocket
Nor threaded through a needle nor tied in a knot
Nor reduced to a simple rod

Don't try to scare me

I won't not even grilled nor twice grilled
Neither raw nor salted
I won't not even in a dream

Don't kid yourself
It's not on I won't

4

Get out of my walled infinity
Of the star circle round my heart
Of my mouthful of sun

Get out of the comic sea of my blood
Of my flow of my ebb
Get out of my stranded silence

Get out I said get out

Get out of my living abyss
Of the bare father tree within me

Get out how long must I cry get out

Get out of my bursting head
Get out only get out

5

Harebrained puppets possess you
And I bath them in my blood
Dress them in rags of my skin

I make them swings of my hair
Prams of my backbone
Kites of my eyebrows

I form them butterflies of my smiles
And wild beasts of my teeth
For them to hunt to kill time

A fine sort of game that is

6

Damn your root and blood and crown
And all in your life

Damn the thirsty pictures in your brain
And the fire eyes on your finger tips
And every every step

Be cast into three cauldrons of crossgrained water
Into three furnaces of symbol fire
Into three nameless milkless pits

Damn your cold breath down your gullet
To the stone under your left breast
To the cut-throat bird in that stone

Be cast to the raven of ravens into the nest of emptiness
Into the hungry shears of beginning and beginning
Into the womb of heaven don't I know it

Damn your seed and sap and shine
And darkness and stop at the end of my life
And all in the world

7

What about my rags
Won't you give them back won't you

I'll burn your eyebrows
You won't be invisible to me for ever

I'll mix day and night in your mind
You'll come beating your head on my door

I'll cut off your singing nails
So you can't draw hopscotch through my brain

I'll hound the fogs out of your bones
So they drink the hemlock off your tongue

You'll see what I'll do to you

8

And you want us to love one another

You can shape me from my ashes
From the débris of my guffawing
From my leftover tedium

You can gorgeous

You can seize me by the hair of forgetting
Embrace my night in an empty shirt
Kiss my echo

Well you don't know how to love

9

Flee monster

Even our footsteps bite each other
Bite behind us in the dust
We're not meant for each other

Rockfast cold I look through you
I pass through you from end to end
This is no game

Why ever did we mix the rags up

Give them back what do you want them for
There's no use their fading on your back
Give them back flee into your nowhere land

Monster flee from the monster

Where are your eyes
Over here there's a monster too

Black be your tongue black your noon black your hope
All be black only my horror white
My wolf be at your throat

The storm be your bed
My dread your pillow
Broad your unrest-field

Your food of fire your teeth of wax
Now chew you glutton
Chew all you want

Dumb be your wind dumb water dumb flowers
All be dumb only my gnashing aloud
My hawk be at your heart

Terror your mother be bereft

11

I've wiped your face off my face
Ripped your shadow off my shadow

Levelled the hills in you
Turned your plains into hills

Set your seasons at odds within you
Turned all the ends of the world from you

Wrapped the path of my life around you
My impenetrable my impossible path

Now you just try to find me

Enough chattering violets enough sweet trash
I won't hear anything know anything
Enough enough of all

I'll say the last enough
Fill my mouth with earth
Grit my teeth

To break off you skull guzzler
To break off once for all

I'll be just what I am
Without root without branch without crown
I'll lean on myself
On my own bumps and bruises

I'll be the hawthorn stake through you
That's all I can be in you
In you spoil-sport in you muddle-head

Never come back

13

Don't try any tricks monster

You hid a knife under your scarf
You stepped over the line you tripped me up
You spoiled the game

That my heaven might turn over
That my sun might smash its head
That my rags might be scattered

Monster don't try any tricks with the monster

Give me back my rags
I'll give you yours

The quartz pebble*

The quartz pebble

To Dušan Radić

Headless limbless
It appears
With the excitable pulse of chance
It moves
With the shameless march of time
It holds all
In its passionate
Internal embrace

A smooth white innocent corpse
It smiles with the eyebrow of the moon

*Quartz is found as round white pebbles in Yugoslavia.

The heart of the quartz pebble

They played with the pebble
The stone like any other stone
Played with them as if it had no heart

They got angry with the pebble
Smashed it in the grass
Puzzled they saw its heart

They opened the pebble's heart
In the heart a snake
A sleeping coil without dreams

They roused the snake
The snake shot up into the heights
They ran off far away

They looked from afar
The snake coiled round the horizon
Swallowed it like an egg

They came back to the place of their game
No trace of snake or grass or bits of pebble
Nothing anywhere far around

They looked at each other they smiled
And they winked at each other

The dream of the quartz pebble

A hand appeared out of the earth
Flung the pebble up into the air

Where is the pebble
It hasn't come back to earth
It hasn't climbed up to heaven

What's become of the pebble
Have the heights devoured it
Has it turned into a bird

Here is the pebble
Stubborn it has stayed in itself
Not in heaven nor on earth

It obeys itself
Amongst the worlds a world

The love of the quartz pebble

He fell for a beautiful
A rounded blue-eyed
A frivolous endlessness

He is quite transformed
Into the white of her eye

Only she understands him
Only her embrace has
The shape of his desire
Dumb and boundless

All her shadows
He has captured in himself

He is blind in his love
And he sees
No other beauty
Save her he loves
Who will cost him his life

The adventure of the quartz pebble

He has had enough of the circle
The perfect circle around him
He has stopped short

He finds the load heavy
His own load inside him
He has let it fall

He finds the stone hard
The stone he is made of
He has left it

He feels cramped in himself
In his own body
He has come out

He has hidden from himself
Hidden in his own shadow

The secret of the quartz pebble

He has filled himself with himself
Has he gorged himself on his own tough flesh
Does he feel ill

Ask him don't be afraid
He isn't begging for bread

He is petrified in a blissful convulsion
Is he perhaps pregnant
Will he give birth to a stone
Or to a wild beast or a streak of lightning

Ask him as much as you like
Don't expect an answer

Expect only a lump
Or a second nose or a third eye
Or who knows what

Two quartz pebbles

They look at each other dully
The two pebbles look at each other

Two sweets yesterday
On the tongue of eternity
Two stone tears today
On an eyelash of the unknown

Two flies of sand tomorrow
In the ears of deafness
Two merry dimples tomorrow
In the cheeks of the day

Two victims of a little joke
A bad joke without a joker

They look at each other dully
With cold cruppers they look at each other
They talk without lips
They talk hot air

from SECONDARY HEAVEN (1968)

The yawn of yawns

The stargazer's legacy

His words remained after him
Fairer than the world
No one dares gaze at them

They wait at the turnings of time
Greater than people
Who can pronounce them

They lie on the dumb earth
Heavier than bones of life
Death didn't manage
To carry them off as a dowry

No one can lift them up
No one throw them down

The falling stars hide their heads
In the shadows of his words

A forgetful number

Once upon a time there was a number
Pure and round like the sun
But alone very much alone

It began to reckon with itself

It divided multiplied itself
It subtracted added itself
And remained always alone

It stopped reckoning with itself
And shut itself up in its round
And sunny purity

Outside were left the fiery
Traces of its reckoning

They began to chase each other through the dark
To divide when they should have multiplied themselves
To subtract when they should have added themselves

That's what happens in the dark

And there was no one to ask it
To stop the traces
And to rub them out

A conceited mistake

Once upon a time there was a mistake
So silly so small
That no one would even have noticed it

It couldn't bear
To see itself to hear of itself

It invented all manner of things
Just to prove
That it didn't really exist

It invented space
To put its proofs in
And time to keep its proofs
And the world to see its proofs

All it invented
Was not so silly
Nor so small
But was of course mistaken

Could it have been otherwise

A wise triangle

Once upon a time there was a triangle
It had three sides
The fourth it hid
In its glowing centre

By day it would climb to its three vertices
And admire its centre
By night it would rest
In one of its three angles

At dawn it would watch its three sides
Turned into three glowing wheels
Disappear into the blue of no return

It would take out its fourth side
Kiss it break it three times
And hide it once more in its former place

And again it had three sides

And again by day it would climb
To its three vertices
And admire its centre
And by night it would rest
In one of its three angles

Petrified echoes

Once upon a time there was an infinity of echoes
They served one voice
Built him arcades

The arcades collapsed
They had built them crooked
The dust covered them

They left the dangerous service
Became petrified from hunger

They flew off petrified
To find to tear to pieces the lips
Out of which the voice had come

They flew who knows how long
And silly blind things didn't see
That they were flying round the very border of the lips
They were looking for

The story of a story

Once upon a time there was a story

Its end came
Before its beginning
And its beginning came
After its end

Its heroes entered it
After their death
And left it
Before their birth

Its heroes talked
About some earth about some heaven
They said all sorts of things

Only they didn't say
What they themselves didn't know
That they are only heroes in a story

In a story whose end comes
Before its beginning
And whose beginning comes
After its end

The yawn of yawns

Once upon a time there was a yawn
Not under the palate not under the hat
Not in the mouth not in anything

It was bigger than everything
Bigger than its own bigness

From time to time
Its dull darkness desperate darkness
In desperation would flash here and there
You might think it was stars

Once upon a time there was a yawn
Boring like any yawn
And still it seems it lasts

Signs

An intruder

A drop of blood in the corner of heaven

Have the stars perhaps again begun
To divide the blue to bite each other
Or to kiss each other

At the sun's round table
Nothing is said about it

Only the fiery bread is broken
Beakers of light pass from hand to hand
And the dead stars gnaw their own bones

What does the drop of blood want in the corner of heaven
In that one-eyed corner of heaven

A winged pipe

A winged pipe flies around
The streaks of lightning in a vast coil
With a song it tries to lure them somewhere

Is it back to the clouds
Or to another lovelier heaven
Or to earth amongst men

It's become entangled in the tongues of flame
Both song and wings are on fire
And its shadow on the gates of heaven

Doesn't it know some other song

With this it will only enrage the lightning streaks
And won't lure them anywhere

An obstinate bundle

A white formless bundle
Moves over the clear heaven

Constantly with all its strength it rocks from side to side
Tied crosswise with green string
And so prepares its step

Constantly struggling it falls
On to the uncaring soil of heaven
And so marks time

Above it one star keeps silence

Below it another star keeps silence
To its right an old sun philosophizes
To its left a young moon prattles

Why doesn't it just calm down for once
The good-natured thunder from the clear heaven
Will certainly untie it

A homeless head

A severed head
A head with a flower between its teeth
Wandering circles the earth

The sun meets it
It bows to him
And goes on its way

The moon meets it
To him it smiles
And does not stop on its way

Why does it growl at the earth
Can't it return
Or leave for ever

Its flowering lips would know

A condemned dagger

A naked grey-eyed dagger
Lies amid the Milky Way

How it wriggles
In the star dust
Is it thirsty for blood

How it leaps up
Does it want to stab
Its own innocent shadow

And how it flashes its blades
Flashes on all sides
Is it signalling to someone

The processions of stars avoid it
And leave an empty space
In the shape of a heart around it

Where is the most glorious hand
That flung it up there
To take it back again

Burning hands

Two burning hands are drowning
In the depths of heaven

They do not grasp at the star
That is floating around them
And blinking and crossing itself

They are saying something with their fingers
Who can guess
The tongue of fingers in the flame

Solemnly they put their palms together
To signify a roof top

Are they talking of the old house
That they left burnt down
Or perhaps of the new one
That they are just thinking of building

The last cord

A fat gay-patterned cord
Crawls amongst the constellations
And can scarcely get through

At each starry crossroads
It ties itself a knot
To remember all the paths

Its endless end
It ceaselessly draws
Out of the blue womb of heaven

It crawls amongst the constellations
Towards the very heart of the world
And never gets tangled

Dissension

A crowned apple

Take the sun out of your mouth
Night is burying us alive

This is my apple
From heaven it fell on to my tongue
Leave me alone to enjoy it

Open your mouth cipher that dawn may come to us
That the sun may crown us too

Pray that I do not open my mouth
There are no more sweet jobs
In the apple for you maggots

A blue noose

Why do you squeeze our necks with the horizon

I like to have the pleats of heaven
Fall thickly over my thighs

You'll throttle us with that belt

I like your lament for the blue noose
When I am tired and unbelt myself

A high path

Pick up your big foot
You're treading on our thought

I cannot carry my steps
Through you in my arms

Move off our thought
Will bite the stars off the soles of your feet

I cannot sacrifice my path
It leads me through your heads

Hardworking threads

Why do your glances
Stitch up our eyelids

I don't know what the sunbeams
Do behind my back

Why don't you turn your head
To see your glances

I don't know now where my head is
If you need it you find it

Foster brood

Gather up your thunderbolts
That are hatching out under our heart

Why do you not cherish
The young echoes of my words yourselves

Gather them up they'll smash both us
And you to smithereens

Why do you not come on their tail
And fly into my heart

Fertile fire

Cut yourself lengthwise cipher
That we too may stand upright

Have you really grown so much
Playing on my fire

Cut yourself crosswise cipher
That we too may spread our arms

Are you really prepared to fly up
By yourselves to the source of my fire

Free flight

Give us leave to fly away
Out of your palace without foundation

I have forged you into stars
Under the vault of my skull
Fly away who's stopping you

Give us leave to perish
Each flight brings us back to the court

Got you there birds
Cut off your wings
That your flight may be free

Imitation of the sun

Death of the sun father

Three paces from the top of heaven
From the lime in everlasting flower
The old sun stopped

Turned red turned green
Turned round himself three times
And went back to his rising

(So as not to die in our sight)

They say there is a son and heir
Before the golden-eye is born for us too
We shall have taught this darkness to shine

Blind sun

Two lame sunbeams
Lead the blind sun

Morning is seeking his fortune
On the other side of heaven
He isn't at his own doorstep

Midday has fallen low
He's gadding about with the lightning
He's never at home

Evening has gone out into the world
With his bedding on his back
He's begging on some star

With open arms
Only night has come out
To meet the blind sun

Clash at the zenith

A blue sun was born
In heaven's left arm pit
A black sun was born
In heaven's right arm pit

The blue one climbs the black one climbs
Towards the tower in the zenith
Where desolation now resides

We have gone down naked into ourselves

We open up the mole hills
We whisper the secret name
Of our own native sun

The golden tripod from the tower
Has set out in three directions

Preparations for a welcome

We set up a gate
Of our flowering bones
At the way into heaven

We spread half our soul
Up one slope of heaven

We devise a table
Of our petrified hands
At the very top of heaven

We spread half our soul
Down the other slope of heaven

We build a bed
Of our leafy heart
At the way out of heaven

We do all this in the dark
Alone without the help of time

We wonder if these are really
Preparations for a welcome
Or only for a farewell

Midnight sun

From a huge black egg
A sun was hatched to us

It shone on our ribs
It opened heaven wide
In our wretched breasts

It never set
But it never rose either

It turned everything in us gold
It turned nothing green
Around us around that gold

It changed into a tombstone
On our living heart

Foreign sun

Whose head did this one-eyed bastard
Drop out of

Who's he gawping at now
Who's he rolling after
Over the fallow heavens

Why is he sizing us up
He'd just love to burn us to cinders

As if from down here we
Had doused his rabid father
With cold water

He'd better cool off
Heaven's made a mistake

Imitation of the sun

The heart of one of us rose
High into the burnt-out heaven

It moved off along the sun's path
Overgrown with iron weeds
And set behind the charred horizon

We waited in vain for it to return
With the golden apple-bearer
Or at least with twelve fiery branches

Since then we all carry
Our hearts on a heavy chain
Fastened to a faithful rib

Schism

Gluttonous smoke

Why did you abandon me
As the smoke bore me upwards

It was you abandoned us at the bottom
Of your emptied lower cauldron

Why did you not seek me
As the same smoke bore me downwards

It's for you to seek us now on the rim
Of your overturned upper cauldron

Why did you not call to me
As the smoke swallowed me alive

It's for you to call to us now through the ears
Of both lower and upper cauldrons

A cake of ashes

Are you still keeping my fire
That I left you

You left us
A stale cake of ashes

Have you unlocked the sign
Of my gate on the crust

We have unlocked the sign
Of your crossed daggers

Are you eating the golden
Sunflower hidden within it

Your cake has eaten our hands
As we were breaking it

An extinguished wheel

Where were you going so happily
With my fiery wheel of thought

We turned on the spot
With it extinguished round our neck

Where did you get to so happily
With my poor blind wheel

Carried away we drove it
To overtake itself

Where did you vanish to
With my demented wheel

Angry we pulled it off our neck
Together with our head

A fireproof spool

Are you still hanging headless
By one of my black rays

We are hanging in your ancient smoke
By one of our golden threads

Do you still not know in the dark
That my ray has burnt out

We know that the faithful thread
Has unwound from our heart

Do you still not see in the dark
That my ray has snapped

We see that our thread is searching
High above the heart for its spool

A clot of darkness

Do you not recognize the clot
Of my ancient grumous darkness

We are cutting to pieces before it
Innocent goldenhaired remembering

Do you not yearn for its secret
By which it would illuminate you

We are chasing forgetting around it
To bite its own tail

Do you not grasp its circles
Above your empty shoulders

We are afraid lest your clot
Replace our lost head

The fiery sunflower

Whence comes at the top of your spine
The dancing circle of fiery tongues

We were playing tunes on our shinbones
It formed of itself

Whence comes in the midst of your circle
The scorched many-eyed field

We were slapping our thighs
It began to glow hot of itself

Whence comes your hidden sunflower
Whole unbroken uneaten

We found it on our shoulders
In place of our red-hot head

An incandescent kiss

What are you doing without my blue glory
In your soft tower tending to its fall

We are setting fire to our last breath
Above the mouth of your lower cauldron

What are you starting without my start
Behind your bars the bones

We are setting fire to our first loneliness
Below the mouth of your upper cauldron

What are you ending without my end
Behind your chirping bolt

We are dreaming that from the incandescent kiss
We save for ourselves the cauldrons' ears

The lime in the midst of the heart

The song of young truth

Truth sang in the darkness
On top of the lime in the midst of the heart

The sun it said will ripen
On top of the lime in the midst of the heart
If the eyes shine on it

We mocked the song
Seized and bound truth
And murdered it here under the lime

The eyes were busy
Outside in another darkness
And saw nothing

A dragon in the womb

A fiery dragon in the womb
In the dragon a red cave
In the cave a white lamb
In the lamb the old heaven

We fed the dragon with earth
We wanted to tame it
And steal the old heaven

We were left without earth
We didn't know where to go next
We mounted the dragon's tail

The dragon looked at us furiously
We took fright at our own face
In the dragon's eyes

We jumped into the dragon's jaws
Crouched behind his teeth
And waited for the fire to save us

The taming of the dagger

A dagger hung a long time
Squinting above our heart

The severed wings flew up
Out of the lime in the midst of the heart
And tamed the dagger

The wings taught the dagger
In flight to trace
The young sun's face around the heart

The wings took the dagger
Broken down by its lesson
Somewhere high up into the dark

We bowed low
To the lime in the midst of the heart

A fish in the soul

A silver fish in the soul
In the fish a little straw
On the straw a gay patterned cloth
On the cloth three virgin stars

We angled for the silver fish
We were quite famished
The fish scarcely tried to escape

We opened the fish
Out of the fish spilt a little straw

The gay patterned cloth fell apart
And the three virgin stars
Lost their virginity

As for the silver fish
Not even the cats would have eaten it
We were terribly disappointed

It is dark now in our soul

The suffering of the golden tripod

A golden tripod limped
Around our hidden heart
And with its leg dug the darkness

We were afraid it might dig
Under the lime in the midst of the heart

Certainly it wanted to dig out someone
Who had already sat on it
Or someone who would yet sit on it

It limped around the buried secret
Counted over its legs
And dug itself out three graves

We danced the sun dance
Around the lime in the midst of the heart

A dove in the head

A transparent dove in the head
In the dove a clay coffer
In the coffer a dead sea
In the sea a blessed moon

We split open the dove
Smashed the clay coffer
Spilt the dead sea

We waded into the sea
Got to the bottom

Deep below the bottom
We saw the transparent dove
And in it a young moon

We came to the surface

High above the surface
Again we saw the dove
And in it a full moon

We began to drink the dead sea

The lime in the midst of the heart

A flowering lime in the midst of the heart
Beneath the lime a buried cauldron
In the cauldron twelve clouds
In the clouds a young sun

We dug for the cauldron through the heart
Dug out the twelve clouds
The cauldron fled with the sun
From one depth to another

We gaped into the last depth
Deeper than our own life
We threw up the digging

We cut down the lime to warm ourselves
Cold gripped us at the heart

Heaven's ring

The stargazer's death

He had to die they say
The stars were closer to him
Even than people

He was eaten they say by ants
He imagined that stars
Gave birth to ants and ants to stars
So he filled the house with ants

His heavenly harlots they say
Cost him his head
And the rumours are absurd of a dagger
With human fingerprints

He was simply out of this world they say
He had gone to find the sunflower
In which meet the paths
Of every heart and every star

He had to die they say

Heaven's ring

Ring no one's ring
How did you get lost
How fall from heaven somewhere
Rather everywhere than somewhere

Why did you at once marry
Your old your ancient shine
To your young emptiness

They have forgotten both you
And their wedding night

Since then your shine has taken to drink
Your emptiness has run to fat
You are lost again

Here is my ring finger
Settle down on it

Nothingness

Nothingness you were asleep
And dreamt that you were something

Something caught fire
The flame writhed
In blind agonies

You woke up nothingness
And warmed your back
At the dream flame

You didn't see the flame's agonies
Whole worlds of agonies
Your back is short-sighted

Nothingness you fell asleep again
And dreamt that you were nothing

The flame went out
Its agonies received their sight
And they too went out in bliss

Orphan absence

You had no proper father
Your mother wasn't at home
When you saw the world in yourself
You were born by mistake

You have the figure of an abandoned abyss
There's a smell of absence about you
You gave birth to yourself

You run around with fiery sluts
You break your heads one after the other
You jump out of one of your mouths into another
And give new life to the old mistake

Stoop down naked if you can
To my last letter
And follow in its steps

I have an idea orphan-child
That it leads into some sort of presence

The shadow maker

You walk through a whole eternity
Along your personal infinity
From head to heels and back

You shine on yourself
In your head is the zenith
In your heels the setting of your shining

Before the setting you let your shadows
Stretch move away
Work miracles and shame
And bow to themselves

At the zenith you cut the shadows back
To their proper size
You teach them to bow to you
And as they bow they disappear

You walk this way even today
But you can't be seen for shadows

The starry snail

You crawled out after the rain
After the starry rain

The stars of their bones
Built you your house themselves
Where are you carrying it on the towel

Lame time is coming after you
To catch you up to tread on you
Put out your horns snail

You crawl over the vast cheek
Which you will never survey
Straight into the maw of nothingness

Turn aside to the life line
On my dreamed hand
Before it is too late

And bequeath to me
The wonder-working towel of silver

Fugitive stars

You looked at each other stars
Stealthily that heaven should not see
You meant well

You were misunderstood

Dawn found you cold
Far from your hearth
Far from the gate of heaven

Look at me stars
Stealthily that earth should not see
Give me secret signs
I will give you a cherrywood staff

And one of my wrinkles as path
And one of my lashes as guide
To bring you home

More About Penguins

Penguin Book News, which appears every month, contains details of all the new books issued by Penguins as they are published. From time to time it is supplemented by *Penguins in Print* – a complete list of all our available titles. (There are well over three thousand of these.)

A specimen copy of *Penguin Book News* will be sent to you free on request, and you can become a subscriber for the price of the postage – 4s. for a year's issues (including the complete lists).
Just write to Dept EP, Penguin Books Ltd, Harmondsworth, Middlesex, enclosing a cheque or postal order, and your name will be added to the mailing list.

Some other books published by Penguins are described on the following pages.

Note: *Penguin Book News* and *Penguins in Print* are not available in the U.S.A. or Canada

The Penguin Modern Poets